Things
I
Like

1997 Impression
Houghton Mifflin Edition, 1996

Printed in the U.S.A.

ISBN: 0-395-75338-4

456789-B-99 98 97

Things
I
Like

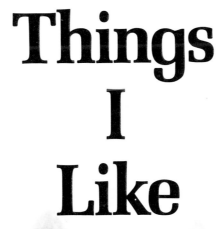

Anthony Browne

HOUGHTON MIFFLIN COMPANY

BOSTON

ATLANTA   DALLAS   GENEVA, ILLINOIS   PALO ALTO   PRINCETON

This is me
and this is what I like:

Painting . . .

and riding my bike.

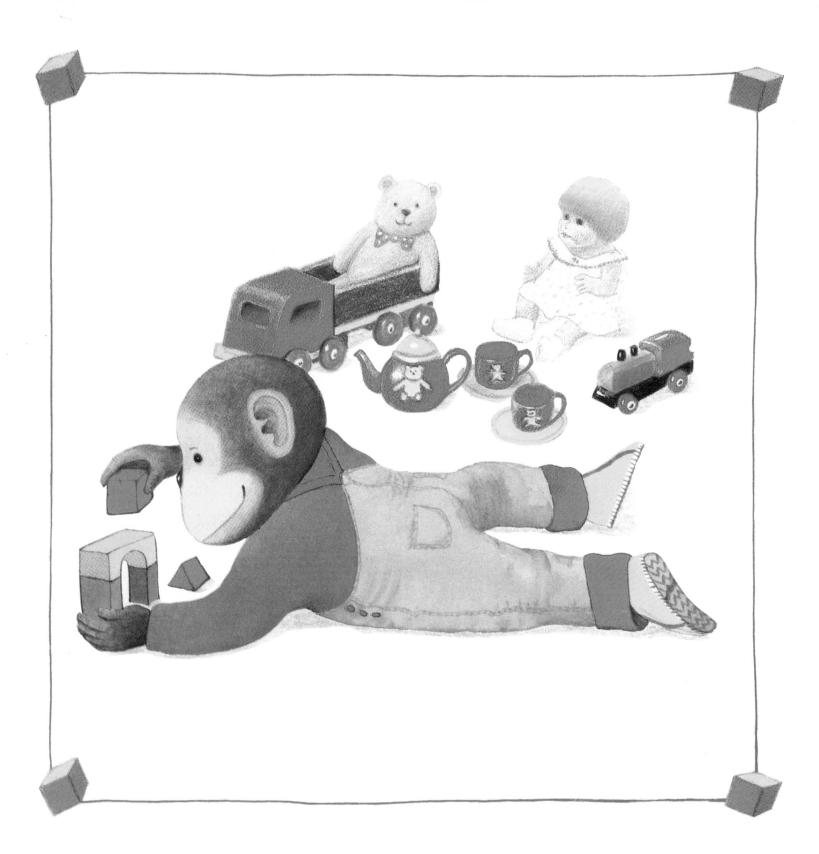

Playing with toys,

and dressing up.

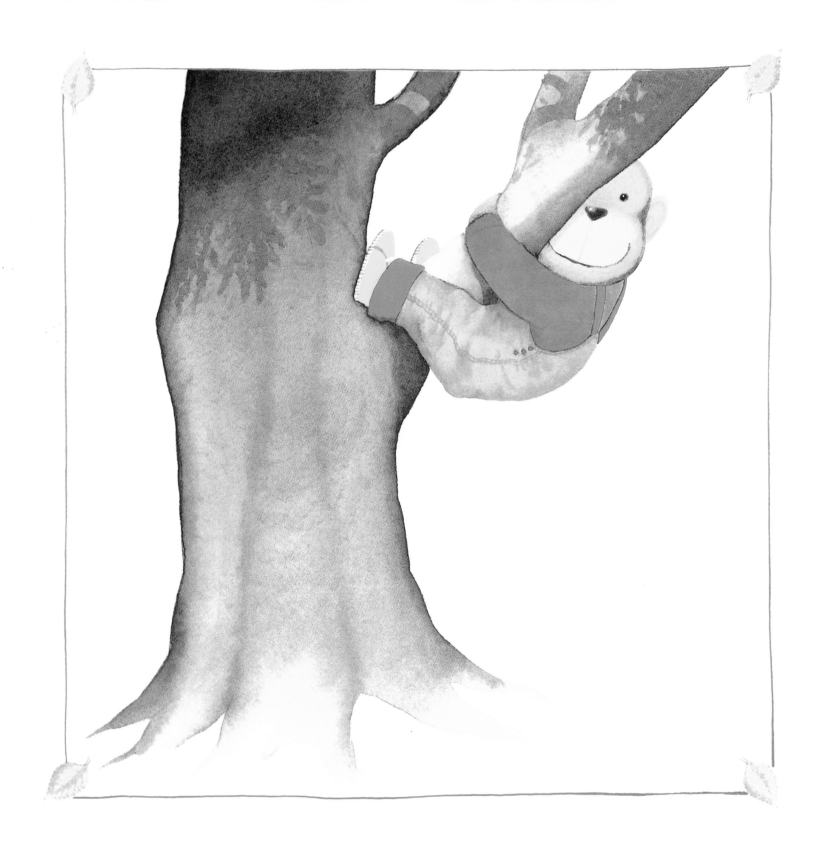

Climbing trees . . .

and kicking a ball.

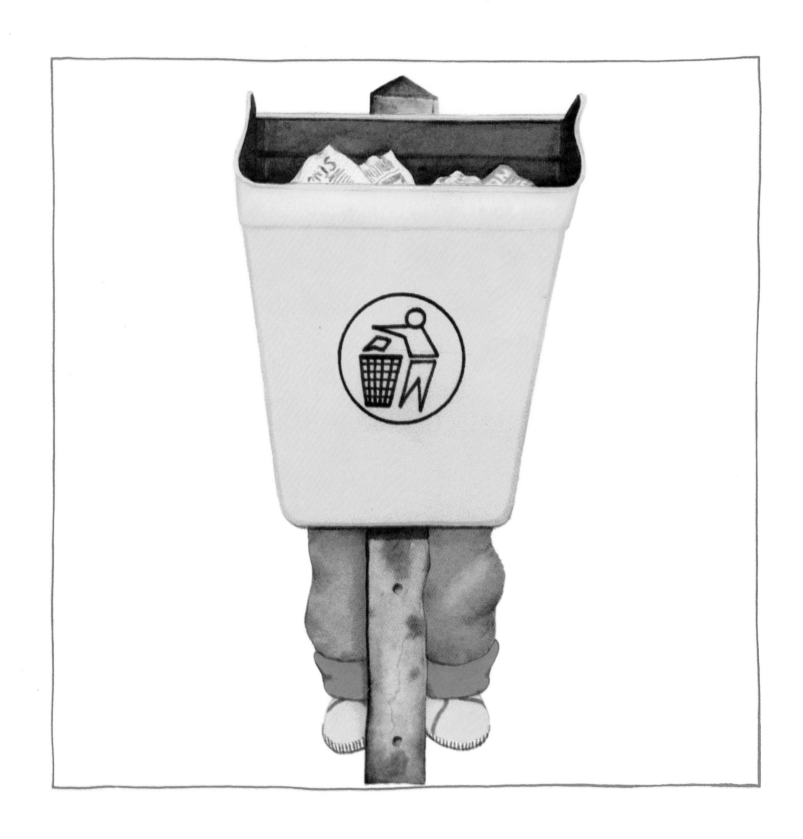

Hiding . . .

and acrobatics.

Building sandcastles,

and wading in the sea.

Making a cake . . .

and watching TV.

Going to birthday parties,

and being with my friends.

Having a bath...

...hearing a bedtime story...

and dreaming.